SCRUM

The Ultimate Beginner's Guide To Learn And Master Scrum Agile Framework

© **Copyright 2018 by <u>HEIN SMITH</u> - All rights reserved.**

The following Book is reproduced below with the goal of providing information that is as accurate and reliable as possible. Regardless, purchasing this Book can be seen as consent to the fact that both the publisher and the author of this book are in no way experts on the topics discussed within and that any recommendations or suggestions that are made herein are for entertainment purposes only. Professionals should be consulted as needed prior to undertaking any of the action endorsed herein.

This declaration is deemed fair and valid by both the American Bar Association and the Committee of Publishers Association and is legally binding throughout the United States.

Furthermore, the transmission, duplication or reproduction of any of the following work including specific information will be considered an illegal act irrespective of if it is done electronically or in print. This extends to creating a secondary or tertiary copy of the work or a recorded copy and is only allowed with an expressed written consent from the Publisher. All additional rights reserved.

The information in the following pages is broadly considered to be a truthful and accurate account of facts, and as such any inattention, use or misuse of the information in question by the reader will render any resulting actions solely under their purview. There are no scenarios in which the publisher or the original author of this work can be in any fashion deemed liable for any hardship or damages that may befall them after undertaking information described herein.

Additionally, the information in the following pages is intended only for informational purposes and should thus be thought of as universal. As befitting its nature, it is presented without assurance regarding its prolonged validity or interim quality. Trademarks that are mentioned are done without written consent and can in no way be considered an endorsement from the trademark holder.

TABLE OF CONTENTS

Introduction 1

Chapter 1 : What Exactly is an Agile Framework? 2

    What is Framework? 2

    What is Agile? 3

    9 Principles of SAFe: 3

Chapter 2 : Agile Manifesto 7

Chapter 3 : What Does Scrum Mean? 9

Chapter 4 : Core Roles In Scrum 12

    The Product Owner 12

    Scrum Master 13

    The Scrum Team 14

Chapter 5 : Non-Core Roles In Scrum 16

    Stakeholder 16

    Vendor 17

    Scrum Guidance Body 17

Chapter 6 : Scrum Artifacts 18

Chapter 7 : Scrum Flow 22

Chapter 8 : Agile Estimation Techniques 24

Chapter 9 : Sprinting In Stages 27

Chapter 10 : Scaling Scrum 34

Chapter 11 : What Is It Good For? Absolutely Everything! 36

Conclusion 42

Introduction

Congratulations on purchasing *Scrum: The Ultimate Beginner's Guide To Learn And Master Scrum Agile Framework* and thank you for doing so!

The following chapters will discuss what exactly Scrum is, the process behind using it, and how it can help you and your business. Scrum can seem very confusing at first, with a lot of little details to remember. This book breaks it down and talks about the most important aspects of Scrum Agile Framework. You'll read about the three main roles of Product Owner, Scrum Master, and the Scrum Team. Each role is integral to the development of the project, and they all have to work together for everything to be successful. How they do that is important and can be a difficult process. However, with the right attitude and focus, each of the three roles can be very efficient and provide quality work. There are other roles involved in the process as well, and each one is as important as the last. And while implementing a framework like Scrum correctly can be challenging, there are different specific stages involved that breaks it down into helpful sections. This book also talks about how Scrum helps the development team, or Scrum Team, to learn communication and cooperation. Learning to succeed as a team is extremely important, and these attributes are needed if the project is to be a success. Not just the team is involved; Scrum Framework emphasizes how important feedback from the customer is because it saves time and money in the long run. Any and all feedback during the development stage is welcome, because it helps the product to be the best possible quality before the end of the project timeline. [Unnecessary repetition].

There are plenty of books on this subject in the market, thanks again for choosing this one! Every effort was made to ensure it is full of as much useful information as possible, please enjoy!

Chapter 1

What Exactly is an Agile Framework?

Scrum Agile Framework. What does that even mean? It sounds like some sort of fancy computer program, something probably that only computer engineers deal with. But is that what it really is? The term can sound a little confusing and complicated, but it's actually much simpler than you might realize!

What is Framework?

Let's start with the basics first. What does "framework" mean? A framework is a term used in software development, and it provides functionalities and solutions to a particular problem area. Basically, it's having the "framework" already there, but then the user (you) come in, and alter it to help you. Think about it like this — you make a cup of tea every morning. You put different ingredients into the cup every time, but you don't measure. So, sometimes there might be more sugar, or other times there might be more of another ingredient. It doesn't bother you that much, because in the end you still get your cup of tea. But then one morning, you think of an idea that could help make things a little more productive. Instead of having all the ingredients separately, you measure out the correct ratio you'd use for one cup of tea and place everything (all the dry ingredients) in one container. From then on, every morning all you have to do is scoop out one spoonful and you'll get the correct amount of everything you'd need for that one cup of tea. It saves time, it makes things easier, and you don't have to do as much work. That's exactly what a framework does. Using computer code, a person can change the framework to suit their specific needs. It helps productivity and makes things easier!

What is Agile?

So what about the term "Agile"? Agile itself means to the ability to move quickly and easily. But how can that be applied to framework? Well, now we know that framework is a computer program that a person can change to help them. So Agile Framework specifically refers to a method of project management, which is used in software development, and is characterized by the ability to turn tasks into short phases of work. Basically, instead of having one long project, the process of Agile Framework is used by breaking down the said project into smaller increments. This allows everyone to focus on one thing at a time, which then helps with quality control. It is based on 9 different "principles", which are used to inform and inspire the roles and the practices of SAFe or Scaled Agile Framework. Scaled Agile Framework is a type of framework that helps you to accomplish tasks in a much easier way. It includes being adaptable and flexible with plans, and has a few different approaches, or principles.

9 Principles of SAFe:

1. Take An Economic View

The biggest reason to use an Agile Framework is because it provides the highest quality product at the best value in the shortest time. However, doing this requires the understanding of the economics of building systems. Every day decisions need to be made in the correct economic context.

2. Apply Systems Thinking

A system is very complex. It has many different components all working together, and each one has defined and share goals. In order to improve, everyone needs to commit to and understand the purpose of the system. Systems thinking should be used in the organization building the system. It has to be used in the future system as well. That is what happens in SAFe.

3. Have Variability In Mind; Ensure That Options Are Preserved

A major sector of design practices favors selecting only one type of design and the qualification options at the beginning of the developmental process. A wrong take-off could have an effect on proposed amendments. This will generate a project design that is becoming too long term.

4. Build Incrementally With Fast, Integrated Learning Cycles

The best way to prevent dealing with a long term project is by developing solutions in a series of short iterations. Iterations build from previous ones and allow for faster customer input, which means less future risks. Iterations can also become prototypes and used in market testing. Early feedback helps to determine when to keep or make any necessary alterations.

5. Let Milestones Be Based On Fair Assessment Of Active Systems

Regular evaluation from the developers, business owners, and customers helps to provide financial, technical, and purpose assurance. They all share the responsibility to ensure that their investment in the solution will actually have economic benefits. So, it's important to have those integration testing points. Doing this provides the milestones in which everyone is able to evaluate throughout the developmental life cycle.

6. Conceptualize And Reduce WIP, Batch Sizes, And See To The Lengths Of Queue

The entire point of using a system like this is to achieve a state of continuous flow and allowing new capabilities within the system to move quickly and visibly. There are 3 keys to help with the workflow:

- ➡ WIP - Work in process; it's important to conceptualize and reduce WIP status, this, in turn, reduces the request for unnecessary changes.

- ➡ Reducing the magnitude of the batches goes a long way in producing fast and reliable flow.

- ➡ Doing something about the length of the queue is a way of hastening the time of fresh tasks.

7. Make Use Of Cadence, Time It With Cross-Domain Planning

Cadence helps to create a certain rhythm and predictability for development. When applied with synchronization, it allows for many different perspectives to be understood, and issues waiting for simultaneous attention and integration. The team is able to operate effectively, even when there is uncertainty during the development of products.

8. Open Up The Inner Encouragement Of Dispensers Of Ideas

Ideas, innovation, and the pursuit of knowledge can't happen with unmotivated workers. Even less so when handing out individual compensation; it causes internal competition and gets rid of the cooperation that is necessary to achieve the larger goals of the system. Providing purpose and autonomy leads to more employee engagement. This results in better outcomes for both the overall enterprise and customers.

9. Decentralize Decision Making

Decentralized decision making is required when needing to achieve fast and valuable delivery. It helps to reduce delays, enable faster feedback, improve developmental flow, and more creative solutions are thought of. When a decision needs to be run by those higher up, many delays can happen in the process. It can cause many setbacks and cost more money. By having everyone involved in the same decision making hierarchy, product development flows quicker for everyone.

So why use Agile Framework? Let's say you've been working on a project for a long time. You're finally finished with it, but the customer decides that they want something else to happen. This means there are many different things you'll have to go back and change, and it wastes time and productivity. Plus money! Using an Agile Framework, and the SAFe principles involves not just you but more people. This includes the customer, the stakeholders, someone in charge of one thing, someone in charge of another, and a developmental team. Doing this means you are able to streamline the work, which saves money, time, and helps with customer input. The project is constantly being worked on during the process and allows for the final product to be done much faster than if there were a bunch of different rewrites.

Chapter 2

Agile Manifesto

While streamlining work is definitely important, the Agile Framework world considers other rules to be much more necessary. There is an emphasis on a sense of community, working together, the customer, and accepting the fact that there will be changes. This means it's necessary to have the ability to go with the flow.

In fact, the Agile Manifesto was created to ensure that others using this program would be doing it for the right reasons.

The four rules in the Manifesto are as follows:

Individuals and interactions over processes and tools

Working software over comprehensive documentation

Customer collaboration over contract negotiation

Responding to change over following a plan

When using the Agile Framework, it's important to remember the above rules, and to implement them into your work. When thinking about them, remembering the utmost target is very essential. This is to meet the aspiration of the clients, and not just with the end product, but throughout early developments. In order to do this, try to welcome various changes, even ones that happen later in the development. Agile Framework uses the acceptance of change in order for the customer to have a competitive advantage. It's also important to deliver working software as often as you can. The range could be anywhere from a couple weeks to a couple months, but there is a strong preference to a shorter time scale. Another important aspect of the Agile Framework is the body of actual developers. Building projects around motivated people makes for better results; so make sure to give them the support they need, along with an environment they can work in, believing in their ability to succeed. The investors and the developers are to cooperate always until the task is achieved to ensure it's completed in the best possible way. After all, the best architectures, requirements, and designs come from self-organizing teams! It's really amazing what a group is able to get done with the right motivation and the right attitude. The team also needs to remember to reflect on how they can become more effective at regular intervals throughout the process. If they figure out a different and better way to do something, then they should adjust their behavior accordingly. When working so closely together, remember that the best communication approach is having a face to face conversation. Tone and reading between the lines can get lost when emailing and speaking over the phone. Many people figure out what someone is talking about through body language. Information is too important, and it can be so easy to misunderstand something when communicating through email.

The technical aspect is also very important to remember; continuous attention to excellence and good design enhances agility. In other words, if you keep putting oil in your car, it'll keep running smoothly. Ignore it and you have to deal with worse things later on. Turning in working software as a sort of "progress report" is a great way to measure said progress and show sustainable development. This allows the stakeholders, developers, and users to maintain a constant pace indefinitely. Using Agile Framework is all about simplicity, and the art of maximizing the amount of work not done.

Chapter 3

What Does Scrum Mean?

So how does Scrum specifically fit into all of this? There are different approaches to Agile Framework; different types that you can use, depending on what fits best with you. It would be like trying on different brands of jeans and picking out the one that feels the most comfortable. Each approach (or type of agile framework) is considered "lightweight", meaning all rules and practices are kept at the bare minimum. Each approach also ensures that the main focus is on empowering developers to collaborate and make decisions together. It's important to note that each developer has a different background, which allows the group to work more quickly and effectively. You don't want everyone to know how to do the same thing. What if they come across a problem that they can't solve because they all have the same background? Having people that can do different things will help to create a more cohesive team, and in turn, the team will create much more amazing things. And remember, the big picture of the Agile development ideology is creating applications in small increments. Each individual increment is tested before being considered complete, which assures the product is built with quality at that specific time, instead of figuring out the quality at a later date.

To summarize, an Agile Framework is a process that the developmental team can follow to ensure positive things happen. It's designed so that all parties, including the customer, can provide feedback while the project is currently being developed. Doing so cuts out problems later on and makes it much more efficient in the long run.

And while the Agile Framework has several different choices for software development approaches, the most popular one is Scrum.

Scrum is a type of Agile Framework that has a broad application, which allows for managing and controlling iterative and incremental projects of all different types. It's useful when there are many different types of projects and helps complete each project in a timely manner while ensuring the value of the product doesn't change. It has a strong collaborative and connective philosophy, which also helps each project to be completed in the best possible way. In order for this to be done, there are different roles in the Scrum process, and each person must take their role seriously. If one person doesn't do their job correctly, then the process will fail. Again, Scrum is all about team-work and connectivity.

Breaking it down even further, Scrum has three basic principles:

Transparency

Inspection

Adaptation

It's all about seeing things how they are and making sure everyone knows what is going on at all times. It's important to be clear and concise and keep everyone informed. You might feel like hiding a mistake, but that will make things much worse in the long run. It's important to be transparent throughout the entire process. Inspection ensures that there is a sort of accountability involved. Each Sprint requires a sort of inspection, so that everything is shown to be on track. Without it, the team could be working on a product that might not even be working! And adaptation is probably one of the most important principles. Things change, that's just how it is in life and in the working world. It's important for the Scrum Team to be able to adapt to all the different changes the process will go through. The customer could change their mind, the Scrum Team could change how they want to complete a task, the Product Owner can easily make changes to the

Product Backlog. Each product goes through so many changes throughout the process, and it's important to be adaptable. Otherwise, the product will fail to be created, and the entire system would have to be reworked.

Chapter 4

Core Roles In Scrum

There are three essential roles in Scrum: **Product Owner**, **Scrum Master**, and the **Scrum Team** (also known as the Development Team). Each of these roles has a specific set of responsibilities that they need to fulfill in order for the project to be a success. They also need to work closely together in a symbiotic relationship for the best possible outcome.

The Product Owner

This is considered to be the "top dog", the "big kahuna", and the "big man in charge". They are the ones in charge and the ones that come up with the big ideas. It's their responsibility to create the vision and work with the Scrum Team to see it done. In fact, no one else is allowed to tell the Scrum Team what to do!

The Product Owner tends to be focused more on the business side of things, representing the customer and stakeholders. The role itself is represented by just one person, since having a team trying to run things would get confusing. It is the Product Owner's responsibility to ensure that the product reaches the highest possible value, which is why they work so closely with the Scrum Team. Both roles working together ensure that everything is done at the right time and that the project is a success.

There are several specific responsibilities that the Product Owner is in charge of. One is managing and building the Product Backlog. The Scrum Product Owner is the only one who can manage the Product Backlog. It's their responsibility to understand, create, and describe when needed the content in the backlog. It's also their role to prioritize the items. This one is especially important because it's the Product Owner's job to know which items need to be seen to first to ensure that every goal is reached in a timely manner and ensure that the Scrum Team understands the specific items in the backlog. Another is Stakeholder Management, which is where the Product Owner speaks with the various stakeholders and is the only one who can do so. The stakeholders discuss different development ideas with the Product Owner, who then passes it on to the Scrum Team in the form of the Product Backlog. The Product Owner is also in charge of Release Management. They come up with the release plan, and at what date everything is due. They are also the one who prices everything since they're responsible for these decisions.

Scrum Master

The Scrum Masters are considered the coaches of the teams. It's their job to ensure the Scrum Team adheres to the values and practices of Scrum, and that delivery flow is optimized. They do everything possible to make sure the Scrum Team stays on task and preforms at the highest level. This includes working with the Product Owner, facilitating meetings, and removing any distractions and impediments to the current progress. A good Scrum Master helps to protect the Scrum Team from over-commitment; it's possible that the product owner will put pressure on the Scrum Team and try to get them to do too much during a sprint. On the flip-side, the Scrum Master also makes sure that the team isn't too complacent and actually does the work they're supposed to get done in a timely manner. It's a fine line, but an extremely important one! A Scrum Master also has to deal with the issue of being in charge but having no actual power over the Scrum Team. They can keep the team on task, and help to facilitate issues, but can't fire or hire anyone. They're there to help the team specifically with Scrum but can only work with the team as members. This means that they can't point out one specific person and have that person do something. The Scrum Master's authority has to be over the team as a whole.

In order to do all these responsibilities effectively, the Scrum Master should be skilled in Coaching, Moderation, and Development Know-how. Each skill will be used in various ways throughout the sprints, and it's important that the Scrum Master is capable.

In the framework, the Scrum Master is also in charge of organizing and running Daily Scrum Meetings, Sprint Planning Meetings, Sprint Review Meetings, and Sprint Retrospective Meetings.

The Scrum Team

The Scrum Team, also known as the Development Team, is the role that completes all the work delivered to the customer. Basically, it's a group of people who work together to deliver the requested product to the client. They have to approach each project with a strong "team" attitude and are a tight-knit group of usually 6 to 10 members. It is possible for there to be many different Scrum Teams, depending on how much work needs to be done. It's important to keep each team in a lower number to ensure the work gets done correctly, but sometimes there is a larger project, which calls for more than one Scrum Team. It's extremely important for all of these teams to coordinate to ensure that everyone is on the same page. In order for this to happen, they have meetings called "Scrum of Scrum Meetings". Each team picks one member, someone to represent them, and all these representatives meet for cross-team coordination. Having someone as the team representative helps them to be even better at working together to get the project done. It's sort of an elite team that reports back to their own respective teams.

Each individual Scrum Team member has a particular set of skills, and they train each other in these skills, so everyone will know what to do. It means that each team is balanced with many different specialties, which the other members need to acquire at least a little bit of knowledge in. Doing this ensures the project doesn't become hindered, and that everyone can help each other with each project. In order for everyone to work together in a proficient manner, each member follows the same rules, has a common goal, and shows respect for one another. As it is when first putting a team together, there might be complications along the way. A new team won't deliver the best possible outcome at first; it takes time to adjust to each other and figure out how to work together. Typically, it takes about an average of 3 sprints before the team works out all the kinks. There are several rules that the members come up with and agree to. This will allow for everything to flow a little more smoothly. They must agree to the time and location of the daily Scrum Meetings, coding guidelines, tools to use, and the "Definition of Done", or DoD, which is used to decide if the work is done or not. If failure does happen, it's never pointed to one specific team member; the Scrum Team is a whole and fails as a whole as well. The best thing the Scrum Team can do to succeed is to define what they'll commit to delivering at the end of the sprint, how each result can be broken down into tasks, and who performs each task and in what order each task is performed.

Each Scrum Team has a specific set of responsibilities that they need to accomplish in order to succeed. They have to perform the daily Sprint Meeting, create the Sprint Backlog, make sure that the product is able to be shipped correctly, and they have to consistently update the status and what remains of their task in order to create the Sprint Burndown Diagram.

Chapter 5

Non-Core Roles In Scrum

Just as there are essential core roles in Scrum, there are also non-core roles. While these roles are not mandatory for a Scrum project and might not even be as involved as the other roles, they are still very important because they can play a significant part in the projects. These roles include the Stakeholder(s), the Vendors, and the Scrum Guidance Body.

Stakeholder

Stakeholder is a term that collectively includes customers, sponsors, and users who frequently collaborate with the Product Owner, Scrum Master, and Scrum Team. It's their job to come up with ideas and help start the creation of the project's service or product and provide influence throughout the project's development. The customer is the specific person who buys the project's product or service. It's entirely possible for an organization's project to have customers within that same organization (internal customers), or customers outside of that organization (external customers). A user is an individual or organization that uses the project's service or product. Just like customers, there can be both internal and external users. It's even possible for customers and users to be the same person. The sponsor is the person or organization that provides support and resources for the project. They are also the person that everyone is accountable to in the end.

Vendor

Vendors are outside persons or organizations. They provide services and products that are not usually found within the project organization. They help bring things in that might not have been there otherwise.

Scrum Guidance Body

The Scrum Guidance Body is optional and is made up of either a group of documents or a group of expert individuals. It's their job to define government regulations, security, objectives related to quality, and other parameters seen in the organization. It's these guidelines that help the Product Owner, Scrum Master, and Scrum Team to carry out their work in a consistent manner. The Scrum Guidance Body is also a good way for the organization to know what the best practices are, and which ones should be used in all Scrum projects. It's important to note that the Scrum Guidance Body doesn't actually make any decisions related to the project. It's instead used as guidelines and a structural way for everyone in the project organization to consult the portfolio, project, and program. It's especially useful for the Scrum Teams, who can look at or ask the Scrum Guidance Body for advice whenever they might need it.

Chapter 6

Scrum Artifacts

What exactly is an artifact? In archaeological terms, an artifact refers to a manmade object, such as a vase or tool. Basically, an artifact is something that we humans make in order to solve a problem or create something. The Scrum Agile Framework uses "artifacts" in order to provide accurate information about the product; what happens while it's under development, the activities being planned, and the activities already done. There are many different artifacts that can be possible in a project, but the main ones are:

1. **The Product Backlog** - A list of all requirements, functions, features, and fixes that are needed to be made to the product for any future releases. As the product is used, feedback is provided and the backlog changes and even gets bigger. It's even possible for the backlog to change completely, depending on technology, business requirements, and market conditions. It's ever evolving; as long as the product exists, so too will the Product Backlog. Typically the items in the Product Backlog have a description, estimate, order, and value assigned to them. It's never a finished list, and constantly changes depending on what the product needs at the moment. The Product Owner is the only one in charge of the backlog, although the team does create something called "Product Backlog Refinement". This is when the Scrum Team adds details, priority order, and estimates to the list, and they decided when and how refinement needs to be done. Normal activities during the refinement include: reviewing the highest priority items on top of the backlog, asking questions to the Product Owner for more

info, deleting items that are not needed any more, writing in new items, prioritizing and ranking the items, redefining the acceptance criteria, refining items to prep for future Sprints, and understanding that the product architecture might change as the backlog emerges. The more detail a product backlog item has, the higher up the list it is. It is necessary to have precise estimates in order to complete the project. So, the less details there means it is lower on the list and will take longer to do. Once the Scrum Team gets more details on an item, they can move it higher on the list.

2. **Sprint Backlog** - The Sprint Backlog can be considered a "to-do" list for the Scrum Team to accomplish. It's the set of Product Backlog items that are selected for the Sprint, plus a plan for realizing the Sprint goal and delivering the Product Increment. Basically, it shows all the work the Scrum Team needs to do in order to meet the Sprint goal. It's a list that is modified throughout the process; whenever new work appears; the Scrum team adds it to the Sprint Backlog. Sometimes things on the Sprint Backlog are deemed unnecessary, so it is possible that different parts of the plan can be removed from the list. Only the Scrum Team can actually alter the Sprint Backlog during a Sprint. It's made specifically for the team and helps them to stay on track and focused. It's considered a real time picture of the work that the Scrum Team plans to accomplish during the Sprint and belongs only to them.

3. **Sprint Burn-down Chart** - Most likely this isn't actually considered a Scrum Artifact. However, this term does show up often enough during the process that it makes sense to keep it on the list. While a Sprint is going on, the Scrum Team can track the total remaining work in the Sprint Backlog. It's the best way to see how long it will take to achieve the Sprint Goal and figure out how to manage the progress. The Scrum Team uses a practice called the Sprint Burn-down Chart as the way to

monitor this progress. The Product Owner takes this information and compares it with previous Sprint Reviews to see if the Scrum Team is on-time and completing their projected work by the desired time for the goal. The Product Owner then shares this information with the stakeholders so that everyone is on board.

4. **Increment** - Considered to be the most important Scrum Artifact, the Increment is when the Scrum Team combines all the Product Backlog items that are completed during a Sprint with the increments of all the previous Sprints. At the end of each Sprint, the Increment must be considered complete, which means it has to be in usable condition and meet the Scrum Team's "**Definition of Done**". Definition of done is a document of shared understanding by the Scrum Team that specifically defines what "done" actually means. This definition can be different for every Scrum Team and tends to mature as the team grows and matures. And even though the Product Owner might decide not to release it, the product must still be in working condition. The members of the Scrum Team are the ones who define what is considered an Increment. Opinions might vary, but team members have to have a shared understanding on what it means for work to be complete in order for it to actually be considered done. They use this information once the task is done. And this information is also used to help the Team to know how many Product Backlog items are selected during Sprint Planning. The Sprint's purpose is to deliver Increments that show the items potential functionality when released, and an Increment of product functionality is delivered with every Sprint. With this information, the Product Owner might choose to release it right away. Each separate Increment is added to all the prior Increments and tested to ensure that all Increments have the ability to work together. And as the Scrum Team spends more time working together, their definition of Increment should

expand to include stronger criteria for higher quality. It's standard practice for all and any products to have an Increment for any work done on them.

The main take- away from this is that the Product Backlog and the Sprint Backlog are used to describe work that needs to be done, work that will add value to the project. The Product Increment is the section of the product that has already been completed during a Sprint. Each of these serves a specific purpose to capture the shared understanding of the Scrum team at a certain point in time. It helps the team to understand how they are doing with the Sprint goal. It also help clear up key information so that everyone has the same understanding across the board.

Chapter 7

Scrum Flow

Scrum Projects can be a lot to deal with. There are many different things going on, and a lot to keep track of. Even the terms themselves can be a little overwhelming! The important thing to remember is that Scrum Projects have 5 essential activities to ensure optimal product development. Using each process will help performance and make things more efficient from the beginning to the very end of the project. This is also referred to as the Scrum Process Flow.

1. **Sprint** - Used by the Scrum Team, a Sprint is a short development period of time where the team creates product functionality. Sprints typically last between 1 and 4 weeks and can even take as little as one day. They're considered to have a short development cycle, so shouldn't take longer than 4 weeks. The planned economic value is determined by how long the Sprint is, so if it takes longer than originally thought, then that means more money spent.

2. **Sprint Planning** - The Scrum Team meets at the beginning of each Sprint, and it is here where they decide and commit to a Sprint Goal. The Product Owner presents the Product Backlog, explains the tasks, and asks the team to choose the tasks they want to work on. The Scrum Team also figures out the requirements that will be used to support said goal and will be used within the Sprint. Plus, the Scrum Team will identify the individual tasks it will take for each specific requirement.

3. **Daily Scrum** - A short, 15 minute meeting that is held every day in a Sprint and includes the Scrum Master. During this meeting, the Scrum Team members coordinate on their priorities. They talk about what is most important to get done during the day, what they completed the day before, and if there are any roadblocks they might run into when doing the current day's work. Doing this helps streamline everything, and prevents any issues popping up unexpectedly.

4. **Sprint Review** - A meeting that is introduced by the Product Owner and takes place at the end of each Sprint. During this meeting, the Scrum Team shows off the working product's functionality that they completed during the previous Sprint to the Product Owner. The Product Owner then determines whether the whole Sprint Backlog is covered or not. It's possible that something might be put back into the backlog if not done correctly.

5. **Sprint Retrospective** - Similar to a Sprint Review, this is a meeting that takes place after each Sprint or project. However, it is not led by the Product Owner, but rather by the Scrum Team themselves, along with the Product Master. They discuss what went well, what possible changes they could make, and how to make those changes. They also discuss how to make the team work more efficient if there were any issues going on. It's important to speak up about issues, otherwise, it could cause problems later on down the road which would prevent the project from continuing.

Chapter 8

Agile Estimation Techniques

Within each Sprint, the team can figure out different ways to decide on an Agile estimation of an item. There is no wrong way, each team should pick whichever one works best for them.

1. **Planning Poker** - Using play cards, the team members write specific numbers on them in order to vote for an estimate. If the votes don't match up, then it continues with a discussion so that everyone is on board; and it keeps going until all the votes are unanimous. This is a good technique when figuring out estimates for a small number of items.

2. **The Bucket System** - This technique uses the same number sequence as Planning Poker, but instead of playing cards, they estimate items by putting them in buckets. The bucket doesn't have to be an actual bucket, the team can use any object that can hold the estimates. This one is actually faster than Planning Poker because there is the phase of divide and conquer. This technique is better for larger numbers than Planning Poker and can estimate a larger number of items as well.

3. **Big/Uncertain/Small** - This is a great technique when the Scrum Team needs a much faster Agile estimation. The items that need estimates are put into three different categories: big, uncertain, and small. The team begins by discussing just a few of them together, and then uses the same divide and conquer technique as The Bucket System to go through whatever is left.

4. **TFB/NFC/1** - This technique is very similar to Big/Uncertain/Small but adds the idea of a specific size to it. The sizing categories are TFB (Too F-ing Big), NFC (No F-ing Clue), and 1 (meaning 1 Sprint or less).

5. **Dot Voting** - A simple and very effective technique that is best when used for estimating only a small number of items. Each team member is passed a small amount of dots and uses them to show the size of the item. The more dots an item has, the bigger the estimate.

6. **T-shirt Sizes** - The team members put the items into t-shirt sizes: XS, S, M, L, XL. This technique is considered a little informal and is good when the information is needed quickly and there is a larger number of items. The sizes are determined with an open and collaborative discussion. If there is a stalemate, then the team can vote on which size they think fits best. Once the estimate is done, the sizes can also be given number values if it's needed.

7. **Affinity Mapping** - This technique is all about putting together the items based on how similar they are. Sometimes there needs to be a discussion on the definition of what similar can mean to the team, in regard to the items. Affinity Mapping works best when there is a smaller number of items, mainly because it's actually a very physical activity. Numerical estimates can be adding to the groupings after everything has been sorted, if necessary.

8. **Ordering Protocol** - Using the very simple scale of low to high, items are put in a random order. Once they're in an order, each team member takes a turn making changes. They can either change the order of an item by moving it one spot lower or one spot higher, they can use their turn to discuss the item in question, or they can pass on their turn. If everyone decides to pass then changing the order is done. This technique also has a

couple of variations: The Challenge, Estimate, Override, and the Relative Mass Valuation method.

9. **Divide until Maximum Size or Less** - The team chooses a maximum size, such as a 1 person day of effort, for each item. They must determine if each item is already that maximum size or is less. If the item ends up being larger than the pre-determined size, then the team breaks up the item into sub-items. The process is then repeated with the sub-items and continues until every item is in the minimum to maximum size range.

In addition to these techniques, there are certain principles to follow when doing an Agile Estimation. The team must remember that the techniques are supposed to be collaborative, which means everyone is involved is included in the process. These techniques also promote a sense of unity; they are designed so that no one person can be blamed for a wrong estimate because it is impossible to trace who estimated what. They are also designed to be faster than normal traditional techniques. Estimation is recognized as a non-value added activity, so these techniques are used to minimize it as much as it possibly can be. Going further into this, Agile estimation doesn't require the estimation of actual dollars or days. Instead, points or labels are used, and items are compared with each other, which avoids the difficulty when comparing something to an abstract concept.

Chapter 9

Sprinting In Stages

Putting together a group of people to accomplish something as sophisticated as the Scrum process can be a difficult task. It is necessary to ensure that everyone is working towards a common goal, and requires a specific process called the Group Development Process. This process is a 5 step program that ensures the Scrum team is as successful as possible. The first 4 stages (Forming, Storming, Norming, and Performing) were developed by Bruce Tuckman in 1965. Tuckman said that these stages are necessary for the Scrum Team to grow and that using this process helps them to face challenges, tackle problems, plan work, find solutions, and deliver the best results possible. Tuckman later added in the final 5th stage (Adjourning) in the year 1977. It's interesting to note that, specifically in Agile software development, teams will exhibit a behavior called "swarming". This is a performance shown as the team comes together, collaborates, and focuses on solving a singular problem. This behavior is adapted from when a swarm of insects is focused on a common event, such as a swarm of wasps attacking a person because said person decided it would be wise to hit the wasp's nest with a baseball bat.

Using the Group Development Process method leads to maturity and a highly efficient Scrum Team. It's necessary to remember that sometimes a process like this can take time. Most companies are more concerned with immediate results and jumping into tasks right away, without thinking about how important team building is. Using a method like this will lead to positive impacts and the Scrum Team's success.

1. **Forming Stage** - It is very important to get the Scrum Team off to a successful start. This stage is used for the team members to get to know one another and find out different things they have in common. They use it to connect in a way that will allow them to work together seamlessly. If this step is skipped, the team might find it difficult to move through the later steps of the process. One way for the team to connect with each other is by doing fun ice breakers. Team members can share personal information; movies they like, their favorite music, or their favorite foods. There might be another team member who likes the same things, which will help them to connect to each other. Also during this stage, the team members are relying on a group leader for guidance and direction. The members are looking for acceptance from the group and want to feel like it's a "safe space". They're looking to keep things simple and wanting to avoid controversy, which means typical serious topics and feelings are avoided. Orientation also plays a big part in this stage. Team members try to become more oriented to not just each other, but the tasks as well. Usually, discussions are revolved around figuring out the scope of each task, how to approach it, and similar concerns. In order for the team members to grow from this task to the next, they must step out of their comfort box, and risk the possibility of conflict.

2. **Storming Stage** - Storming is an apt name for this stage. This one is the most likely to have arising conflicts and competition. The "fear of failure" or "fear of exposure" might come into play and increase the desire for structural clarification and commitment. Members will question who is going to be in charge, who is responsible for what, what the rules are, the reward system, and what the criteria for evaluations are. There might even be behavioral changes in attitudes based on issues of competition. Team members might ally with other team members, especially ones that they are already familiar with. It is even possible that cliques might form, which some of the

team members would be against. Some members might feel more comfortable speaking up, while others would feel it was better to remain silent. It could end up with the Scrum Team feeling splintered and not as if they are a team. It's important to figure out different working styles and other obstacles that are standing in the way of the group completing their goal. The best way to solve conflicts is through a collaborative and problem solving based approach. It's the only way for team members to unify and work together. The only reason for skipping a step like this is if the Scrum Team is already established and has been working together for a while. It's possible they already know each other's working style and are already banded together as a team. If this step is needed, then the only way for the Scrum team to move to the next one is by adopting a problem solving mentality. And the most important trait for each member to have is the ability to listen.

3. **Norming Stage** - This stage is all about cohesion within the group. It's important for each member to acknowledge each other's contributions, community building, and attempt to solve the group issues. Team members must be willing to change their previous ideas and opinions when presented with facts from other team members. This should go along with asking questions of each other. The team acknowledges that leadership is shared, and there is no need for any cliques. Having all the members get to know each other and identify with each other is important in strengthening trust. which then contributes to the development of the group as a unit. It's also important to have established rules for how the team operates in each meeting. The team members need to discuss logistics, such as location of the meeting, how long the meeting will take, and what time it starts. They need to talk about how the meeting will flow, and what to do if conflicts happen. Inclusion plays an important role within the Scrum Team. Every group member needs to feel like they belong, so that they actually participate in all the

activities. The main goal is to find a set of rules that everyone can agree to, and then actually follow. Doing this will help the team to operate as the best they can be. The group will feel a sense of camaraderie and almost a feeling of relief when the interpersonal conflicts are resolved. In this specific stage, creativity is high; there's a sense of openness and sharing of information, both on a personal and task level. Everyone feels good about being part of a group that gets things done. The only drawback at this stage is that the members resist change of any kind, and the ones that fear the inevitable future breakup of the group. They may decide the only way to avoid said breakup is by resist forming it in the first place.

4. **Performing Stage** - This stage is not reached by all groups. If they have reached it, the group has formed a tight knit team that trusts each other and is ready to perform tasks efficiently and effectively. Team members are able to work independently, in subgroups, or as the group as a whole with equal productiveness. Everyone's roles are able to change and adjust depending on the needs of the group and individuals. This is the stage where the group is the most productive. Each individual member has become self-assuring and feel as if it's unnecessary to seek group approval. Team members are both task-oriented and people-oriented. There is a certain feel of unity and. Group morale is high, group loyalty is strong, and everyone knows who they are as a group. Products that the Scrum Team works on can change over time, so there is a strong feel of support for experimentation in solving issues. The team is capable of working together well enough to adapt and accept that change. Everyone knows that the overall goal is productivity reached through problem-solving and hard work. Performance is also best if the team follows the rules set in the Norming Stage because it's used to solve personal conflicts. If such a situation occurs, the team would need to review the rules and enforce what the team originally decided on.

5. **Adjourning Stage** - This stage wasn't originally a part of the process and was added in later years. But just because it was added at a later time, doesn't mean it is any less important! At this point in time, the team has most likely fulfilled the project vision. While the technical sides of things are done, the team needs to check in with things on a more personal level. They need to reflect on how they worked together as a team and see if there are any improvements that could be made. The team also recognizes participation and achievements. They can also use this as an opportunity to say personal goodbyes. The team worked closely with one another on an intense project. It's important to wrap things up on a personal level, otherwise there could be a feeling of incompleteness. And what if the team gets back together in any future projects? It's important that they discuss the process and methodologies that succeeded and the ones that failed. The team can go through and decided if there was anything that could be salvaged with a little bit of change. Information gathered during this time might even be used for performance evaluations. So, it's important that the team takes this stage seriously.

Sometimes it can be difficult to follow the stages. There could be a person that is especially stubborn, or maybe some people just don't particularly work well with others. In order for the group to reach its best potential, they must be flexible enough to accept when they need help. There are a few different steps that a group can take to ensure they develop properly through the different stages:

1. The group needs to make sure they change up the responsibility of group facilitator. Each person should have a chance to be "in charge" and doing so creates a feeling of inclusion and equality.

2. The purpose and mission of the group needs to be clear to all members involved. And the mission should be looked over often, just in case anything has changed or any member has

forgotten what it originally was supposed to be. It's entirely possible the mission changes, depending on what the customer's feedback is after a Sprint. Keeping the mission statement updated will help everyone to stay on task.

3. Rules are very important and need to be established and monitored throughout the entire process. Having the rules helps everyone know where things stand and what to do if a rule is broken or in question.

4. The group should remember that conflict can be a positive thing and is completely normal. The conflict could even be necessary for the group's development. One member might disagree with another on how to complete a task. Because of the two members disagreeing, they might actually invent a third way to complete said task that is much more efficient.

5. The group should remember to listen to each other. Having one person to speak over everyone isn't productive and can cause the group to be upset or resent each other. If everyone remembers to listen, then everyone feels as if they are heard by the other members. People tend to respond better and are more accepting of other's if they feel as if they've had the chance to be heard.

6. Each session should end with constructive criticism instead of harsh "advice". It's important to lift each other up and be helpful towards each other, instead of putting each other down. And it's also important to remember that the constructive criticism should be about the group process and nothing personal.

7. Everyone should contribute and do the work. Having one person do all the work makes said person feel resentful toward the whole group. And if only one person is doing the work, then it's entirely possible that the product won't be finished on

time and any deadlines will be behind schedule. The same thing goes for one person sitting out while the rest of the group does all the work. That one person will get credit for work they haven't done, and it's not fair to the rest of the team.

Chapter 10

Scaling Scrum

Scrum was first introduced as a method used mainly for smaller projects. Many believed that's all it was good for but didn't really know if it was possible to scale Scrum because it's never been done before. So how can Scrum even be scalable? It actually is possible, through something called Scrum of Scrum Meetings. This was spoken about a little bit in Chapter 4, but this chapter will dig a little deeper into how Scrum Teams actually work.

Scrum Teams ideally have between 6 and 10 members. However, if there is a need for more than 10 people, then multiple teams are formed. This is fantastic for larger projects and requires open communication and synchronization between each team. Each team picks a representative, who then meets with all the other representatives. They update each other about progress, different challenges being faced, and coordinate activities. How often Scrum of Scrum Meetings take place is determined by the size of the project, how complex the project is, inter-team dependency, and the recommendations of the Scrum Guidance Body.

So how do the meetings work? It's recommended that the teams have face to face communication between them. However, this isn't very often possible, since many companies have various teams working in different time zones and locations. If this happens, then social media and video conference calls can be used. These meetings, called the Convene Scrum of Scrums Process are run by the Chief Scrum Master and helping the Chief are representatives from various teams, who are usually the Scrum Master of their individual teams. For the especially large projects, involving many different teams, having numerous meetings may be necessary. And because it can be difficult to have everyone together at the same time, it is vital that all important matters be discussed whenever the meetings take place. However, before the meetings even take place, the Chief Scrum Master announces the agenda, which the individual teams can then look at and think about any other items that need to be discussed. And any issues, changes, or even risks that have the possibility of affecting the many teams should be brought up and talked about during the meeting. Even challenges facing the individual teams should also be brought up, because there's always the possibility of it affecting multiple teams.

The individual representative from each team should update the other teams. When doing so, it's best to follow these 4 guidelines: What work has my team done since the last meeting? What will my team be working on until the next meeting? Is there anything that remains unfinished that the other teams were expecting to be done? and Will what we're doing affect the other teams?

The most important rule about Scrum of Scrum Meetings is ensuring that there is excellent coordination across the different Scrum Teams. There are many instances of tasks that involve inter-team dependencies; meaning one team's task may depend on another team's delivery of another task. So, it is vital that each team is open in their communication and everyone works together. Doing this ensures the best possible results without any issues along the way.

Chapter 11

What Is It Good For? Absolutely Everything!

So, what exactly is Scrum good for? What can it be used for, and why even use it? What is the purpose, and is it even worth using it?

There are several reasons to use Scrum and implementing it into your business is definitely a smart idea. Think about the competitiveness factor. The market changes faster and faster every day, and only those who are flexible and contemporary can keep up with it. Using Scrum, a person can stay competitive and create a unique advantage for themselves. And the best part is that it's not some unproven fad! It's a solid and successful Agile Framework that has been proven again and again across various projects and teams. College universities use it to deliver projects to clients. Militaries rely on Scrum to prepare their ships for deployment. Even in the automotive world, a car is being built by using Scrum! And not just any car; one that is fast, affordable, efficient, safe, and should sell for less than $20,000!

Scrum also allows the development of features and gives the customer the ability to stay involved. The customer is able to receive working versions throughout the process, see the progress that is being made, and even add new ideas if necessary. All of that is important because waiting until the end of the project to show the customer could potentially be a huge mistake. They might hate the final version, and request a complete do-over, which is a waste of time and money. Think about it like this — if you're getting your hair cut, do you watch the process of your stylist, or do you close your eyes until it's all over?

Unless you want to be surprised and don't really care about the end result, you naturally keep an eye on what the stylist is doing. If they start cutting your hair too short or dying it a funky color, you speak up and ask them to stop and/or rework it. You don't want to end up with terrible hair that you hate! Using Scrum Agile Framework is all about transparency; a clear vision for all involved. It also allows for all of the stakeholders to be informed, which specifically helps discover weaknesses and makes for more effective teamwork. Scrum allows everyone in the loop during a project, which means there are fewer mistakes to be made.

Quality also plays a big part in Scrum. Testing is something that happens at every Sprint, which means it happens often; usually daily! Doing this secures the quality of every product from the beginning on and allows for problems to be recognized and fixed on time and promptly.

It also helps with costs, which is something every business likes to hear. Each project usually has a fixed period, which means there's a definitive cost involved and it won't get any higher. And while the effort and little details might change thought out the process, the cost will always remain the same since the period of a project is definite.

Something the customer would really love about Scrum is that changes are always welcome! They can be shown to the Product Owner at any time, who then follows through with them in the next Sprint meeting. The Product Owner informs the Scrum Team, who then implements the changes as soon as the next day. Doing this helps the customer get the product they desire, and a happy customer is always good for the company.

Scrum can also help with efficient communication skills and creativity. It involves everyone within the project and requires strong communication, collaboration, respect, and understanding. A successful project is built off of what the customer requires and what the team develops, and Scrum can help enforce both of those. Those in the Scrum Team especially benefit from acquiring communication skills. They develop these skills over stages, and by the end of the process are able to communicate effectively. This can be used in both the professional and personal life.

The development of complex systems and extensively long projects can be difficult and very frustrating. Luckily, Scrum can help with the exact planning needed for these types of projects, which allows for the integration of new functionalities and a new way of thinking. Using Scrum will help things to run smoothly and won't allow for a terrible realization at the end of the project that something has gone wrong. It basically streamlines the process and makes it better for everyone involved.

A good thing to also point out is that using Scrum is just plain fun! It's all about team work, collaboration, and making decisions together. It can be fun to work closely in a group; you get to know others on a personal level and might even make new friends out of it! Apart from that, it's a fantastic way to use your creative side and really get in touch with learning new things. You're able to bounce new ideas off each other, and truly feel as if you're contributing to something special. Using Scrum is implementing the best part of software development, which is a creative and multi-faceted activity that works best when everyone is doing their share.

There are also several instances when Scrum can help a business in very specific ways. After all, maybe your business is doing just fine, and you think it doesn't need a change. However, consider this — organizations that implement Scrum experience changes in their companies culture. They become more team oriented, more value oriented, and place more value on the customers themselves. Would you rather work for a company that cares only about profits, or work for one that cares more for its people? Businesses using Scrum teams become high performance and show results that are much higher than normal teams.

What about the other side of things? Instead of a business that's doing just fine, let's say there's an organization that could be in deep trouble, but they're willing to adopt the Scrum system. Adopting a new system shakes the company up, and allows for a new culture, process, and team environment, which then helps the business actually get out of trouble. The business completely changes around, and people actually want to start working there. The most important thing about this scenario is that the business is willing to admit they actually need the help! Sometimes organizations don't like to admit there are things wrong, which leads to bad things for the business. Using Scrum, they can get back on their feet, and back to where they would like to be.

Another way Scrum can help a business is when there is a small business that has a high performance state but is struggling to maintain said high performance when they're also trying to grow all at the same time. They can easily implement Scrum in their organization, and it will help immensely in balancing things out. Scrum can help steam line their production so they're not so overwhelmed with everything all at once. The organization helps immensely and makes it seem like things are easier to accomplish.

It's not just businesses and companies that benefit from using Scrum; anyone who has a complex project can use it! It could be someone who is working on a new smartphone app, someone who is overseeing a store or charity event. Scrum a great way to prioritize to-do lists into tasks that are actually manageable, helps to improve teamwork, improves communication skills, and creates faster results. When using Scrum, a person becomes agiler (pun intended!), they discover how to react more quickly and how to respond better to changes that inevitably come their way. All it needs is the ability to stay focused, the ability to collaborate with others, and the ability to communicate successfully. Doing all these things allows a person to accomplish what they need to get done in a way that is beneficial to all.

If none of the above reasons convinced you, here are 7 different reasons to use Scrum:

1. **Perfect Implementation** - Scrum has a defining set of roles, activities, artifacts, and rules. Using everything together, you get the ability to implement your ideas in a way that seems almost perfect! As long as every role and rule is followed, then the project becomes an amazing streamlined process.

2. **Easy to use** - Scrum is very easy to use and can be introduced into an organization with minimal hassle. Although there are several roles and different regulations to follow, one person isn't' taking on all that responsibility. It's spread evenly throughout the entire group, which makes doing your job super easy!

3. **Flexibility** - Scrum is an adaptable practice. Sometimes you don't always start with all the information, and gather it along the way, which Scrum is really good for. Changes can be introduced during the next Sprint and implemented into the process.

4. **Reduces Risk** - Scrum reduces project risk by creating in increments. In doing so, development cost is reduced, and the risk of starting over is lessened.

5. **Optimize Team Efficiency** - Scrum is all about a team that works together and gets things done. By following the correct stages and resolutions, the Scrum Team becomes an unstoppable force capable of creating many different ideas.

6. **Customer Can Use the Product Before It's Actually Released** - At the end of every Sprint meeting, a Sprint Review is done. This is where the customer is introduced to new changes and new features within their product. This part of the project is usable to the customer, so they can inspect the work

and try it out. Doing this helps lessen the work that needs to be done at the end of the process and ensures quality control.

7. **Continuously Improving** - When one project is done, the Sprint Retrospective meeting happens. That is when the Scrum Team meets up and discusses any constructive criticism or issues that might have happened during the project timeline. By figuring out the issues at this moment, they can prevent any future ones of the same natures from happening again.

Conclusion

Thanks for making it through to the end of *Scrum: The Ultimate Beginner's Guide To Learn And Master Scrum Agile Framework*. Let's hope it was informative and able to provide you with all of the tools you need to achieve your goals whatever they may be.

The next step is to try and integrate Scrum into your business or company! It's an amazingly useful process that can truly help streamline your work ethic. It can help you work on your communication skills, learn how to be a team player, and jump start your creative side. It doesn't have to be used in a high-end company; it could even be used for running a charity event! It's a program that is extremely effective and flexible, and definitely worth doing.

And while there are many different moving parts within this process, it's actually not too difficult. Each role has something different to focus on and splitting up the jobs helps things run more smoothly. Scrum is all about making work easier, and it definitely accomplishes that! And even though the work becomes easier, the quality of the product goes up. It's a win-win! By working on the product in different increments, and including the customer throughout the entire process, quality is assured and there is no need to go back and fix it after everything is done. Obviously using Scrum is the best choice and will really help you to in your business or personal ventures.

Finally, if you found this book useful in any way, a review on Amazon is always appreciated!

Made in the USA
Las Vegas, NV
26 March 2024